THIS BOOK BELONGS TO:

_____

Welcome to Cambodia! This beautiful country is in Southeast Asia, and it's full of wonders. Cambodia is known for its ancient temples, tropical forests, and kind-hearted people. The country is shaped like a jewel, and its flag has a very special picture on it – Angkor Wat, the world's largest temple!

Cambodia's most famous place is Angkor Wat, a giant temple that was built almost 900 years ago! It's so big, it's like a city! People come from all over the world to see it. It was built by a king and is a special symbol of the country.

Most people in Cambodia follow a religion called Theravada Buddhism. It teaches kindness, peace, and respect for all living things. You can find beautiful temples, called pagodas, all across Cambodia. Inside, people pray, meditate, and offer flowers and incense to show their respect. Monks in orange robes help guide people and live simple lives focused on learning and helping others.

The people of Cambodia are called Khmer. They speak the Khmer language, and they love sharing stories, food, and music with others. Cambodians are known for being friendly and always smiling. Family and community are very important to them.

Cambodians wear beautiful traditional clothes for special occasions. Women often wear a colorful silk dress called a sampot, and men wear silk shirts and sarongs. You'll see bright colors like red, gold, and green. These outfits are perfect for dancing, celebrating, or going to the temple.

One of the biggest celebrations in Cambodia is Khmer New Year! It happens in April, and everyone gets together to have fun. People play games, throw water to cool off, and visit temples to pray for good luck. Homes and streets are decorated with bright flowers and lights.

Cambodia is home to exciting festivals. One of the most special is called the Water Festival, or Bon Om Touk. It happens every November and celebrates the end of the rainy season. People race boats, light lanterns, and have big celebrations by the river.

Cambodian music is full of rhythm and melody! Traditional Khmer instruments like the roneat (a wooden xylophone) and skor thom (big drums) create beautiful sounds. Musicians play these instruments during festivals, ceremonies, and performances. People love to listen and dance along to the music, especially during celebrations like weddings and New Year.

Have you ever seen a dance that tells a story? In Cambodia, traditional dances like the Apsara dance do just that! The dancers wear beautiful, sparkling costumes and gold crowns, and every movement of their hands and feet means something special.

Cambodian markets are full of life! You can find all kinds of things: fresh fruits, tasty snacks, and handmade toys. The best part is the delicious street food, like fried noodles and sweet treats. People walk around, chatting and laughing while shopping for the day.

Cambodian food is delicious! You might try Amok, a yummy dish made of fish and coconut milk, or Bai Sach Chrouk, which is pork and rice. They also love fruits like mangoes, bananas, and dragon fruit. Cambodians enjoy sharing food with their friends and family.

In Cambodia, kids go to school just like you! They learn about math, reading, and their country's history. Some schools are in big cities, while others are in small villages. The students love to play games during breaks, especially soccer and tag!

Cambodia has its own unique alphabet called the Khmer script. It's one of the oldest alphabets in Southeast Asia and has 33 letters! The letters are curvy and look like art. Children in Cambodia learn how to read and write Khmer when they start school. Writing in Khmer is like drawing beautiful patterns with every letter!

In Cambodia, the rainy season lasts from May to October. The rain helps grow rice and other crops, which is very important for Cambodian farmers. During the rain, children splash in puddles and play with paper boats. After the rain, everything is green and fresh!

The Mekong River flows through Cambodia, providing fish, water, and life to the people. Villages are built along the riverbanks, and boats drift along carrying fishermen and farmers. The river is full of surprises – even rare freshwater dolphins!

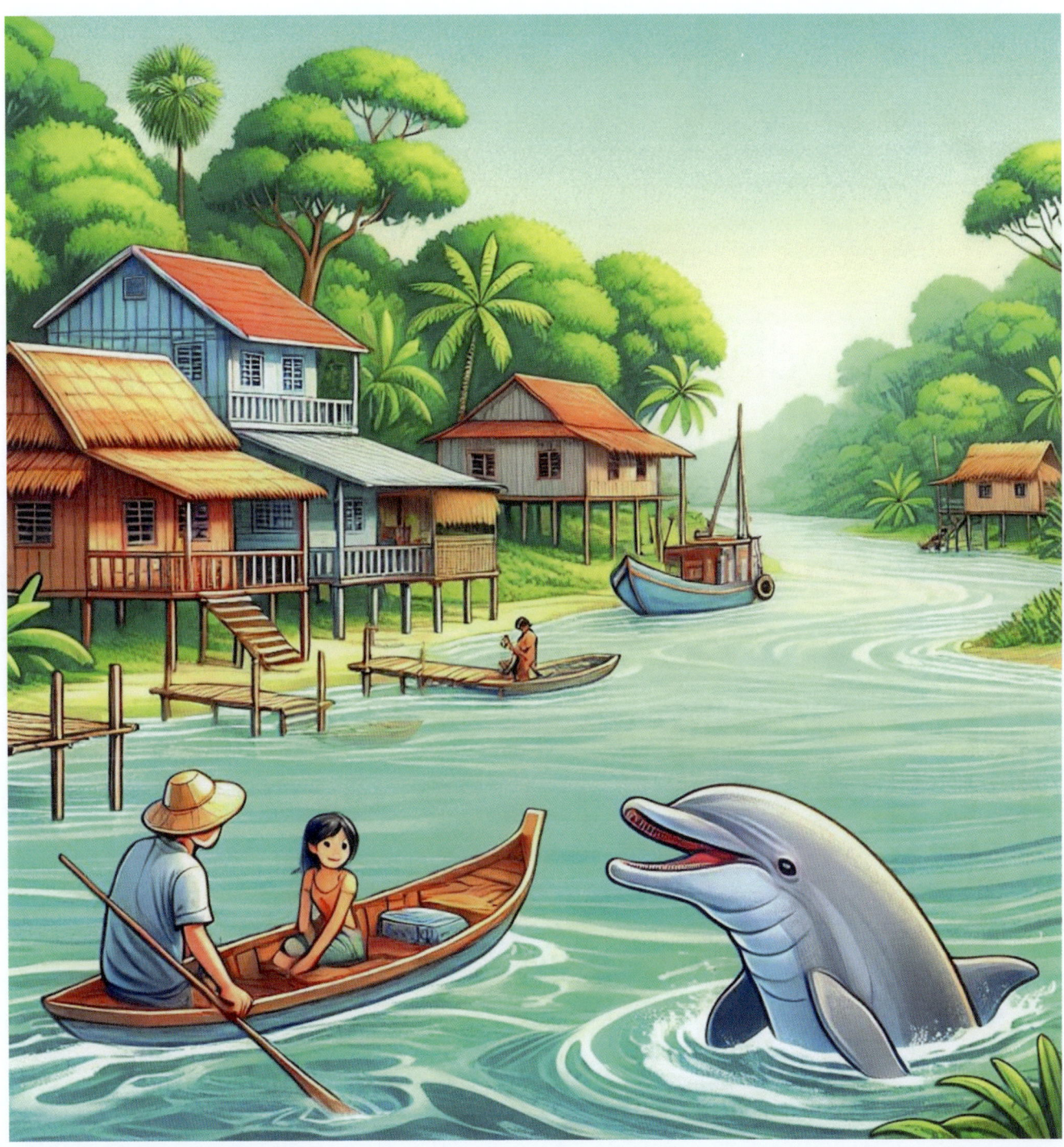

Cambodia is home to many amazing animals. In the forests, you might spot tigers, monkeys, and colorful birds. There are also beautiful butterflies everywhere! In the rivers, crocodiles and turtles swim, while in the mountains, rare animals like clouded leopards live in secret.

In Cambodia's jungles, elephants roam! Elephants are very important in Cambodian history. They were once used in royal parades and helped build temples by carrying heavy stone blocks. Now, they are protected and cared for by special conservation groups.

Now you know all about Cambodia's amazing culture, places, and people. There are so many wonderful things to see and do in Cambodia. Maybe one day, you'll visit and experience this magical country for yourself!

Printed in Great Britain
by Amazon